THE POOH COOK BOOK

THE POOH
COOK BOOK

INSPIRED BY **WINNIE-THE-POOH** AND

THE HOUSE AT POOH CORNER BY A. A. Milne

By Virginia H. Ellison

Illustrated by Ernest H. Shepard

A YEARLING BOOK

Published by
DELL PUBLISHING CO., INC.
1 Dag Hammarskjold Plaza
New York, New York 10017

Yearling ® TM 913705, Dell Publishing Co., Inc.

Reprinted by arrangement with
E. P. Dutton & Co., Inc.

Printed in the United States of America

Third Printing— May   1974

Grateful acknowledgment is made for permission to adapt the recipe "Pennies from Heaven" from *The Honey Cookbook* by Juliette Elkon, © Copyright 1955 by Alfred A. Knopf, Inc. Reprinted by permission of the publisher.

For Jim
and
Dave, Jan and Nick

Acknowledgments

I am deeply grateful first to my mother for all she taught me and to Mrs. Elaine Minick who, at 82, is still a great baker and whose recipe suggestions were no less valuable to me than her encouragement. I owe much to Mrs. Brian Mahoney, a professional English cook and to her daughters, Siobhan, Kerry, Nicola, and Moira, especially for the lucky day when I was staying with the girls and we were experimenting with honey and discovered how beautifully it took food color.

I found the publications of the American Honey Institute, Chicago, Illinois, very helpful, though no recipes from them were used.

I thank Akeita Somersille for the *Hipy Papy Bthuthdth Thuthda Bthuthdy Cake I* on page 88 which she made especially for us when she knew we were doing this book; and Beryl Barrow for dozens and dozens of facts and hints from her vast knowledge of cooking.

To the following good friends who were also faithful testers and tasters, I am forever grateful:

Mrs. Thomas Falk and her daughter, Heidi; Mrs. Michael DuBissette and her five daughters, Linda, Deidre, Gloria, Elaine, and Fay; Mrs. Raymond Buckley and two of her five children, Blake and Lisa, who were often on loan to me after school and as tactful as Pooh and Piglet in letting me know when something wasn't up to standard.

Mrs. Marvin Barrett read the manuscript. She and her daughters, Elizabeth and Mary Ellin, helped me with excellent suggestions, editorial and culinary.

Mrs. Mary Shaw, who knows good food from garden to

table, typed the manuscript and gave me valuable advice of all kinds as she went along.

Thanks, too, to the late Elliott B. Macrae, President of E. P. Dutton & Co., Inc.

Contents

THE POOH COOK BOOK

Introduction

This may be—and probably is—the only cook book in the world with interchangeable recipes. If you like something very much for breakfast or as a smackerel, there's no reason why you may not have it for lunch or tea or supper another day. If you had, say, Poohanpiglet pancakes at breakfast, you could add a little something to them for lunch—blueberries or strawberries, perhaps—or put a little something special on them for supper—grated orange rind and minted honey beaten into a little cream, for example.

In other words, you don't have to eat breakfast recipes only at breakfast, or smackerel and tea ones only at smackerel or teatime. If something's delicious, there's no rule to say you may eat it only at one certain meal.

Recipes using honey appear in this book only a little less often than Pooh eats or talks about it. The other recipes are for some of his friends, such as Piglet, Eeyore, and Christopher Robin. But mainly they're for you. As a cook, you should know that honey is almost twice as sweet as sugar, and yet when you eat it, it doesn't make you want to go on eating sweets. Honey is also healthful, and very good for active people. When used in cooking it keeps food moist and adds a flavor all its own, as you will see when you've made some of the dishes in *The Pooh Cook Book*. Clover honey is the best all-purpose honey, but there are as many flavors, or kinds, of honey as there are blossoms on flowers and bushes and trees.

Each recipe has a quotation accompanying it from *Winnie-the-Pooh* or *The House at Pooh Corner*. If you've never read these books, why not start at the beginning of *Winnie-the-Pooh* and read the ten chapters in it, one at each meal, and then the ten in *The House at Pooh Corner*? Then, when you use *The Pooh Cook Book* you can play a game of Guessing-Which-Chapter-the-Quotation-Comes-From.

The Pooh Cook Book is particularly useful for special occasions, real or invented, and meant to make what might be an ordinary day into a festive one—almost as good as a birthday or a holiday. A small amount of imagination can turn the simplest dish into a party dish to celebrate the first day of school or the last, losing a first tooth, a rainy day in summer, the first snow of winter, or the first snowdrop or crocus or violet of spring.

All the recipes have been tested more than once. Most of them are simpler to do if you have a sister or a brother or a friend who can measure out ingredients; butter muffin tins and cookie sheets; chop nuts in a chopping bowl; pick nasturtium leaves; run outdoors in the country to catch a bowl of snow; count out loud the number of cups or spoons of anything; shape cookies and candies; decorate cakes and pies; help lick spoons and bowls; be a tester and taster of samples of everything.

When you've read the quotations and cooked and eaten the dishes in this book, we hope you will feel as Pooh did when he answered the question Christopher Robin asked him:

"What do you like doing best in the world, Pooh?"

"Well," said Pooh, "what I like best—" and then he had to stop and think. . . . When he had thought it all out, he said, "What I like best in the whole world is Me and Piglet going to see You, and You saying, 'What about a little something?' and

Me saying, 'Well, I shouldn't mind a little something, should you, Piglet,' and it being a hummy sort of day outside, and the birds singing."

We hope it will be a hummy sort of day inside whenever you use *The Pooh Cook Book*.

Virginia H. Ellison

BREAKFASTS

"When you wake up in the morning, Pooh," said Piglet, "what's the first thing you say to yourself?"

"What's for breakfast?" said Pooh.

Winnie-the-Pooh

Marmalade on a Honeycomb

2 1-inch squares cut from   Marmalade, ginger or plain
  a honeycomb

Spread the honeycomb squares lightly with the marmalade.
Chew.
Do not swallow the beeswax.

At breakfast that morning (a simple meal of marmalade spread lightly over a honeycomb or two) he
had suddenly thought of a new song.

Winnie-the-Pooh

Poohanpiglet Pancakes

(*Yield: about 16 small pancakes, using 2 Tablespoons of batter*)

Use a pancake mix and follow the directions on the box or make your own with:

1 cup all-purpose flour
1 teaspoon baking soda
½ teaspoon salt
1 Tablespoon sugar

1 cup sour cream or milk
or
½ cup sour cream and
½ cup sweet milk
2 eggs
2 Tablespoons shortening, margarine or butter
½ cup fresh or canned wild blueberries, drained (optional)

Rub your pancake griddle or frying pan with the cut half of a turnip, or grease it with a little shortening or margarine. If you use butter, use half butter and half shortening or margarine.

Sift together into a bowl the flour, baking soda, salt, and sugar.

Melt the shortening and set aside to cool.

Stir in the sour cream or milk, or the mixture of sour cream and milk, beaten with the eggs.

Add the shortening.

Beat the mixture until smooth, by hand or in an electric mixer.

If you like small thin pancakes, add a very little more milk or water.

Pour 1 Tablespoon of the batter onto the hot griddle as a

test pancake to see if the griddle is the right heat. Bubbles should appear in less than a minute. When the pancake bubbles all over, flip it and brown the underside. Peek under it by lifting one edge of the pancake with a spatula to see if it is brown. Adjust the heat under the griddle, so that the pancakes come out golden.

Serve with any of the honey sauces, honey butter, plain honey, or syrup.

Try the pancakes with different kinds of honey.

"I've been finding things in the Forest," said Tigger importantly. "I've found a pooh and a piglet and an eeyore, but I can't find any breakfast."

The House at Pooh Corner

Scrambled Eggs

Put water in the bottom of a double boiler and set on medium heat.

Butter the inside of the top of a double boiler generously.

Allow one egg for each person to be served. Whisk the eggs together in a bowl with a little cold water, about 2 teaspoons for each egg.

Pour the eggs into the top of the double boiler and put it into the bottom of the double boiler. Stir with a fork or a long-handled spoon as the eggs begin to set. Add salt and pepper.

For a special breakfast, remove the top of the double boiler from the bottom just before the eggs are the texture you want and add a little butter or cream.

Crisp bacon crumbled into eggs scrambled this way makes a very good brunch dish.

Some hours later, just as the night was beginning to steal away, Pooh woke up suddenly with a sinking feeling. He had had that sinking feeling before, and he knew what it meant. *He was hungry.*

Winnie-the-Pooh

Popovers for Piglet

(*Preheat oven to 425°F*)   (*Yield: 8–12 popovers*)

1 cup all-purpose flour
½ teaspoon salt
¾ cup milk

2 Tablespoons honey
1 Tablespoon melted butter
  or margarine
2 large eggs

Grease the muffin tins.

Sift the flour and salt together.

Add the milk, honey, and melted butter, and stir to blend.

Beat in the eggs.

Fill each muffin tin just under half full.

Bake 25–30 minutes or until sides are rigid and the top and sides of the popovers are brown.

Do not open the oven for 25 minutes to peek or the popovers will fall and not rise again.

If you like popovers dry inside, slit each with a sharp knife and bake 5 minutes longer.

Serve with honey butter or plain butter.

"I wish Pooh were here. It's so much more friendly with two."

Winnie-the-Pooh

Apricot Honey Bread and Muffins

(Preheat oven to 350° F for bread)   *(Preheat oven to 375° F for muffins)*

1 stick butter or magarine (¼ pound) at room temperature
¼ cup honey
⅔ cup mashed, canned apricots
1 large egg

1 Tablespoon canned apricot juice
2 cups sifted all-purpose flour
½ teaspoon salt
2½ teaspoons double-acting baking powder

Grease and lightly flour 1 loaf pan, 8″ long, 2½″ deep, and 4½″ wide, or 2 muffin tins (12 muffins, 2⅜″ diameter, medium).

Cream the butter with the honey and add the mashed apricot pulp.

Beat in the egg and the apricot juice.

Sift flour, salt, and baking powder together. Fold into the mixture.

Fill the loaf pan or the muffin tins about half full.

Bake the loaf in a 350°F preheated oven for 45 minutes to an hour, or until a cake tester, knife blade, or toothpick stuck into the center of the loaf comes out clean.

Bake the muffins for 30 to 35 minutes in a preheated 375°F oven.

Serve hot with honey and butter or honey butter.

"Well," said Pooh, "it's the middle of the night, which is a good time for going to sleep. And tomorrow morning we'll have some honey for breakfast. Do Tiggers like honey?"

The House at Pooh Corner

Minted Honey Banana Bread

(Preheat oven to 350° F)

2 bananas, medium size
¼ teaspoon extract of mint (optional)
3 Tablespoons honey
2 Tablespoons butter, very soft, or melted and cooled
½ cup sugar

2 unbeaten eggs
¼ teaspoon salt
2 cups flour sifted with
1 teaspoon double-acting baking powder and
1 teaspoon baking soda

Grease a loaf pan, 8″ by 4″.

Mash the bananas; there should be about 1 cup. Add the extract of mint, the honey, butter, sugar, eggs, salt.

Mix them by hand or in an electric mixer until well blended, for 3 minutes or longer.

Resift the flour with the baking powder and soda and gently fold into the mixture. Turn into the loaf pan.

Bake 45 minutes in the preheated oven until a knife blade or a toothpick comes out clean when stuck into the middle of the loaf, or when top springs back when gently pressed with flat of knife blade.

Let the loaf stand for a minute before turning it out of the pan onto a rack to cool.

Serve hot, or toasted, with butter and honey. Also good for smackerels, lunches, teas, and suppers. And cold to take on Expotitions.

"Come along and we'll go and see Kanga. She's sure to have lots of breakfast for you."

The House at Pooh Corner

Muffins, Plain or Blueberry

(*Preheat oven to 400° F*)

(*Yield: 12 medium, 2⅝″ diameter*)

1½ cups all-purpose flour
2½ teaspoons double-acting
    baking powder
½ teaspoon salt
¼ cup sugar
¼ cup butter

3 Tablespoons honey
¼ cup milk
1 large egg, beaten

½ cup of blueberries
    or huckleberries
    (optional)

Grease the muffin tin or tins.

Sift and combine the flour, baking powder, salt, and sugar.

Over low heat melt the butter and the honey. Stir together.
Remove from the heat and add the milk. Beat in the egg.

Combine the two mixtures, stirring only until moistened.
Stir in the blueberries.

Fill the muffin tins half full and bake for 20 minutes or until
a toothpick stuck in the center of a muffin comes out clean.

Eat with fresh butter.

Pooh put the cloth back on the table, and he put
a large honey-pot on the cloth, and they sat down to
breakfast.

The House at Pooh Corner

Making Butter

(Yield: ½ cup sweet butter)

½ pint heavy cream   5 cups ice water
1 bowl   1 wire strainer
1 rotary beater   1 large spoon

Let the cream stand in the bowl at room temperature for an hour.

Put on an apron or an old blouse. Then beat the cream with the rotary beater. When butter curds form, strain off the buttermilk.

Continue beating until the cream is butter and can be beaten no longer.

Put the butter in the strainer and pour the ice water over it.

Put the butter back in the bowl and work it with the back of the spoon until the last of the buttermilk can be poured off.

This is sweet butter. If you prefer salt butter, stir in ½ teaspoon of coarse salt. If you would like to make honey butter, add ½ cup of honey to ½ cup of butter. Stir them together.

"What shall we do about poor little Tigger?
If he never eats nothing he'll never get bigger."
The House at Pooh Corner

SMACKERELS,
ELEVENSES,
AND TEAS

"Nearly eleven o'clock," said Pooh happily. "You're just in time for a little smackerel of something . . .

The House at Pooh Corner

Honey Hot Chocolate
for a Very Blusterous Day Outside

FOR 1 CUP: ¼ cup water
                   Pinch salt
              1 Tablespoon unsweetened cocoa

Stir and simmer for 2 minutes until smooth.

Add: 1 Tablespoon honey
         ¾ cup milk

Heat but do not boil.

FOR 4 CUPS: ⅓ cup water
                4 Tablespoons unsweetened cocoa
                2 pinches salt

Stir and simmer for 2 minutes until smooth.

Add: 2 Tablespoons honey
         3 cups milk

When it is very hot and before it boils, remove from the heat and serve.

"Correct me if I am wrong," he said, "but am I right in supposing that it is a very Blusterous day outside?"

The House at Pooh Corner

Honey Milk Punch
for a Friendly Day

(Yield: 6 cups)

6 eggs
¾ cup honey (½ pound)

1 quart milk
1 whole nutmeg (½ teaspoon ground)

Beat the eggs until foamy and pour the honey into them gradually. Wild rose honey is lovely for this, if you have it.

Grate a whole nutmeg, or stir ½ teaspoon of ground nutmeg, into the milk and heat it over low heat until beads form around the edge.

Do not boil.

Spoon a Tablespoon or two of the nutmeg milk into the egg-honey mixture and stir. Slowly add the rest of the nutmeg milk, stirring all the time.

Set out cups or mugs with big handles and snow white paper napkins. Fill the cups and sprinkle a little nutmeg on top. Good for a midmorning or midafternoon party.

If any punch is left, pour it into custard cups.

Fill a pan with about 1 inch of water and set the custard cups in it.

Bake in a preheated 325° F oven for one hour or until the custard is set.

"Let's go and see *everybody*," said Pooh. "Because when you have been walking in the wind for miles, and you suddenly go into somebody's house, and he says, 'Hallo, Pooh, you're just in time for a little smackerel of something,' and you are, then it's what I call a Friendly Day."

The House at Pooh Corner

Honey Berry Lemonade

(Yield: 6 generous cups)

4 large juicy lemons*
½ cup or more of honey*
1 sprig mint for each glass
1 pitcher

3½ cups water
1 cup mulberries, raspberries,
blackberries, boysenberries,
or strawberries

Squeeze the lemons and stir in the honey gradually. Taste to see if it is the right sweetness. When the honey and lemon juice are thoroughly combined, add the water and the mulberries or other berries in the pitcher.

Pour into glasses that have been frosted in the freezer and are half full of ice. Decorate each glass with a sprig of mint.

* If you use frozen lemonade, then add a Tablespoon of honey for flavor after you add the amount of water required on the package.

"Gaiety. Song-and-dance. Here we go round the mulberry bush."

"Oh!" said Pooh. He thought for a long time, and then asked, "What mulberry bush is that?"

Winnie-the-Pooh

Homemade Snow and Honey

2 Tablespoons honey, warmed   1 tray ice cubes

If you have an ice crusher, crush the ice cubes to a powdered snow.

By hand: put the ice in 2 or 3 plastic bags and cover with a double fold of foil. Hammer until the ice is a powdery snow.

Pour the warm honey over the snow and eat.

The more it
SNOWS-tiddely-pom,
The more it
GOES-tiddely-pom
The more it
GOES-tiddely-pom
On snowing
The House at Pooh Corner

Lemon /
Raspberry Ice Punch

(Yield: 8 generous servings)

FOR LEMON PUNCH:
1 cup of honey lemonade (page 36), frozen in mold
1 cup of pineapple juice
1 quart of ginger ale

Slide the frozen lemonade into the pineapple and ginger ale mixture in a punch bowl. Float mint leaves, violets and young violet leaves on top.

(Yield: 8 generous servings)

FOR RASPBERRY PUNCH:
1 pint of raspberry or lemon sherbet, softened and packed into a
   1-pint mold.
1 cup of raspberry juice or syrup or cranberry juice, chilled
1 cup of peach juice or peach or apricot nectar, chilled
1 quart of ginger ale, chilled
   Handful of raspberries (optional)
   Few sprigs of fresh mint

Pour the raspberry and peach juice into a punch bowl.
Syrup and nectar are both sweeter than juices, if you like a
sweeter drink. Add the ginger ale.

Slide the frozen raspberry mold into the bowl.

Strew a handful of raspberries into it and float a few sprigs of
fresh mint on it.

> Sing Ho! for a Bear!
> Sing Ho! for a Pooh!
> And I'll have a little something in an hour or two!
> *Winnie-the-Pooh*

A Very Nearly Tea

One 4-cup earthenware teapot

I

5–6 carrot tops, feathery leaves

Orange honey

or

Honey with a few drops of orange juice

or

Honey and a small piece of fresh or dried orange peel

II

5–6 sprigs of parsley

Lemon honey

or

Honey and a slice of lemon

or

Honey and a piece of lemon peel

Fill a 4-cup earthenware teapot with hot water and set it on an asbestos pad to warm.

Fill the tea kettle with cold water and bring to a boil.

Wash the carrot tops or parsley.

When the teapot is warm, spill out the water and fill the teapot with carrot tops or parsley. Twist them so that they are thickest at the bottom of the teapot.

Pour boiling water onto the carrot tops or parsley and fill the teapot.

Let it steep for at least 20 minutes.

For carrot-top tea, put orange honey in a teacup before pouring in the carrot-top tea.

For parsley tea, put lemon honey in the teacup.

Serve with lightly buttered curls of Fairy Toast.

Christopher Robin was at home by this time . . . and he was so glad to see them that they stayed there until very nearly tea-time, and then they had a Very Nearly tea, which is one you forget about afterwards . . .

The House at Pooh Corner

1 loaf of bread, unsliced. This is a good way to use up stale bread.

Cut thin shavings off the loaf.

Arrange loosely, not touching, on a cookie sheet.

Bake in a slow oven at 250° F until crisp, lightly brown, and slightly curled. Time varies depending on the freshness of the bread. Usually with stale bread, it takes about 15–20 minutes.

. . . for, Owl, wise though he was in many ways, able to read and write and spell his own name WOL, yet somehow went all to pieces over delicate words like MEASLES and BUTTERED TOAST.

Winnie-the-Pooh

Ginger Ale and Ice Cream

1 glass ginger ale

1 large scoop ice cream

1 teaspoon honey

1 iced-tea spoon

Put the scoop of ice cream in a tall glass. Spoon the honey over it. You may stir ice cream and honey together or leave as is. Add ginger ale.

Drink and eat.

It was a warm day, and he had a long way to go. He hadn't gone more than half-way when a sort of funny feeling began to creep all over him. It began at the tip of his nose and trickled all through him and out at the soles of his feet. It was just as if somebody inside him were saying, "Now then, Pooh, time for a little something."

Winnie-the-Pooh

Oatmeal Wafers

(*Preheat oven to 350° F*)   (*Yield: 4–5 dozen*)

1 cup rolled oats	½ teaspoon baking soda
to make	¼ cup honey
1½ cups of oat flour	¾ cup of liquid shortening
1½ cups of all-purpose flour	or vegetable oil
(unbleached is very good)	¼ cup of water, or less
¼ cup sugar	¼ cup of rolled oats, unground
1 teaspoon salt	2 large cookie sheets

Grease cookie sheets.

Grind the rolled oats in an electric blender to a fine oat flour. If you have no blender, put the rolled oats in a plastic bag and cover with a double thickness of foil. Hammer the rolled oats to a fine flour.

Sift the all-purpose flour with the sugar, salt, and baking

soda. Add the oat flour. Stir in the honey and liquid shortening until all are mixed.

Add the water gradually and only enough of it to make a stiff dough.

Divide the dough into two balls.

Roll each ball in turn to a thickness of ⅛ inch on a lightly floured board or between sheets of wax paper.

Dust the top with rolled oats and press the oats into the dough with a rolling pin.

Cut the dough into small squares, rectangles, triangles, stars, or other shapes, even Pooh shapes, and put them on the greased cookie sheets.

Bake about 15 minutes or until lightly brown.

Dust for Cookies: dust with sugar and cinnamon.

Let cool on a rack.

Winnie-the-Pooh came over all funny, and had to hurry home for a little snack of something to sustain him.

Winnie-the-Pooh

Honey Toffee Pennies

¼ cup (2 ounces) butter, sliced
¾ cup honey
1¼ cups brown sugar, firmly
   packed
1 Tablespoon cider vinegar
1 heavy-bottomed saucepan
1 after-dinner coffee spoon
   or
1 quarter-teaspoon
   measuring spoon

Choose one of these flavorings
for each batch of toffee:
6–7 drops extract of mint
      or
¼ teaspoon of one of these:
   powdered cinnamon,
   nutmeg, ginger
      or
Juice of ½ lemon

Put the butter, honey, sugar, and vinegar in the heavy-bottomed saucepan. The saucepan must have a heavy bottom or the toffee will burn.

Keep over low heat until mixture has melted.

Stir and increase the heat.

Boil without stirring at high heat for

         10 minutes for chewy toffee;
         15 minutes for hard toffee;
         20 minutes for brittle toffee.

Add the flavoring when you remove the saucepan from the heat, while candy is still boiling.

Honey toffee tastes good at every stage, so it doesn't matter whether you boil it for ten minutes or more. What matters is not to stir it.

Drip the honey toffee from a small spoon in penny shapes onto a dish or a piece of plastic or Pliofilm or wax paper. If you are very clever, you will be able to drip it from the spoon in all kinds of shapes—clouds and snails and beetles and birds as well as Pooh shapes.

Or you can drip it from the spoon in small blobs and wait until it cools, so that you can shape it with your hands into balls or little squares or rectangles.

A good trick to keep the toffee liquid is to put the saucepan with the toffee in a larger pan of hot water. You won't have to work quite so fast if you keep the toffee hot and liquid.

The 15- and 20-minute toffee gets harder the longer it sits. When hard enough, wrap in plastic or wax paper and store in an airtight container.

"And the only reason for making honey is so as *I* can eat it."

Winnie-the-Pooh

Honey Toffee Apples

1 recipe for Honey Toffee Pennies, page 46, boiled for 15 minutes on high heat	8–10 small apples, chilled 8–10 lollipop sticks (tongue depressors, which you can buy in the drugstore)

Wash and dry the apples. Remove stems. Push the lollipop sticks firmly into the stem end of the apples.

Remove the toffee from the heat and let it cool a few minutes before dipping the apples in it.

Dip the apples one at a time into the honey toffee and whirl them over the saucepan, turning the lollipop stick round and round in your hand.

As the toffee hardens on the apple, run it under ice cold water from the kitchen faucet and keep twirling.

When they have hardened, which they do quickly, stand the apples stick end up on a dish or foil or wax paper to finish cooling and hardening.

"Many a bear going out on a warm day like this would never have thought of bringing a little something with him."

Winnie-the-Pooh

Easy Honey Buns

(*Yield: 6–8 buns*)

1 package hot roll mix
    or
1 pan buns or rolls ready
   to brown in the oven
	2 Tablespoons chopped
	   peanuts or other nuts
	¼ cup honey

Follow the directions on the mix or for browning the buns.

Combine the peanuts and honey. Stir until the chopped nuts are evenly distributed.

Two or three minutes before the buns are ready, take them from the oven and brush the honey-nut mixture over them. Return to oven.

It's very, very funny,
'Cos I *know* I had some honey;
'Cos it had a label on,
    Saying HUNNY.
        Winnie-the-Pooh

Cream Scones

(Preheat oven to 400° F)   (Yield: enough for 4 at tea)

1¼ cups sifted all-purpose flour
2½ teaspoons double-acting
    baking powder
¼ teaspoon salt
3 Tablespoons butter

½ teaspoon honey
    or
1 teaspoon sugar
1 large egg
¼ cup light cream

Sift the flour with the baking powder and salt.

Cut the butter into the flour with a pastry blender or two knives until it looks like coarse meal.

Stir the honey or sugar, the egg and cream together. Add to flour mixture. Beat well but do not overwork.

Pat the dough on a floured board or between sheets of wax paper until about ½-inch thick.

Cut it in rounds, squares, triangles, or, if you are very clever, make tracings of Pooh and Piglet and the other animals and cut around the tracings.

Bake on a cookie sheet for 10 minutes. Serve hot with sweet butter that you have made, page 29, or with honey butter.

"Hallo, Owl," said Pooh. "I hope we're not too late for——I mean, how are you, Owl?"

The House at Pooh Corner

PROVISIONS
FOR PICNICS
AND EXPOTITIONS

"Oh! Piglet," said Pooh excitedly, "we're going on a Expotition, all of us, with things to eat. To discover something."

Winnie-the-Pooh

Watercress Sandwiches

6–8 sprigs watercress,
    washed and dried
  1 hard-cooked egg

1 Tablespoon mayonnaise
1 teaspoon milk

Chop the egg into coarse pieces in a chopping bowl.

Add the leaves and thin top stems of the watercress to the chopped egg and continue chopping until fine.

Moisten with the mayonnaise thinned with the milk. Add more milk to a firm spreading consistency.

Spread 6 slices of bread with mayonnaise and cover 3 of them with the watercress-egg mixture. Top with the other 3 slices.

Wrap them in plastic wrap or put them in sandwich bags.

Now it happened that Kanga had felt rather motherly that morning, and Wanting to Count Things—like Roo's vests, and how many pieces of soap there were left, and the two clean spots in Tigger's feeder; so she had sent them out with a packet of watercress sandwiches for Roo . . .

The House at Pooh Corner

Radish Sandwiches
with Bread and Butter Prickles

---

1 small bunch young red
    radishes, washed and dried
6–8 bread and butter pickles

Mayonnaise
Sandwich bread or crackers

Grate the radishes and moisten them with mayonnaise to a firm spreading consistency.

Spread the mixture on thin slices of sandwich bread or crackers.

Sprinkle with bread and butter pickles cut in prickle shapes.
Prickle shapes: $\triangle$ $\triangle$ $|$ $/$
Without the prickles these taste and look a little like lobster salad.

"What's the matter?" asked Pooh.

"*Hot!*" mumbled Tigger.

"Your friend," said Eeyore, "appears to have bitten on a bee."

Pooh's friend stopped shaking his head to get the prickles out . . .

The House at Pooh Corner

Ham and Cheese Sandwiches
with Honey Mustard

¼ cup mild mustard   1 Tablespoon honey

Combine the mustard and honey in a large bowl and let them sit while you make the sandwiches. You may add more honey or more mustard to suit your taste.

6 slices boiled or baked ham,   12 slices sandwich bread,
  cut in bite-size pieces   rye is very good
6 slices Cheddar, Swiss, or other   Butter
  mild cheese, cut in small
  pieces

Butter the bread.
Spread the ham and cheese with honey mustard on 6 slices of the bread.
Cover with the other slices.

"I think," said Christopher Robin, "that we ought to eat all our Provisions now, so that we shan't have so much to carry."
"Eat all our what?" said Pooh.
"All that we've brought," said Piglet, getting to work.

Winnie-the-Pooh

Deviled Eggs

6 hard-cooked eggs
½ teaspoon salt
⅛ teaspoon pepper

3 Tablespoons heavy cream
or mayonnaise thinned
with cream
Paprika
12 parsley flowerets

Shell the eggs. Cut in half lengthwise and put the yolks in a bowl.

Mash the yolks and add the heavy cream or the thinned mayonnaise, the salt and pepper. Mix thoroughly.

Fill the yolk cavities with the yolk mixture. Pile in a mound on top. Shape with the tines of a fork.

Sprinkle with paprika. Decorate each with a floweret of parsley.

". . . And we must all bring Provisions."

"Bring what?"

"Things to eat."

"Oh!" said Pooh happily. "I thought you said Provisions. I'll go and tell them."

Winnie-the-Pooh

Cucumber or Mastershalum-
Leaf Sandwiches

4 thin slices of peeled cucumber
for each sandwich
    or
4 small nasturtium leaves,
if you live in the country and
grow nasturtiums

Salt and pepper
Cream cheese or mayonnaise

Spread the sandwich bread with cream cheese or mayonnaise.

Arrange thin slices of cucumber or the nasturtium leaves on the mayonnaise on half the bread slices. Add salt and pepper to taste on the cucumber slices.

Put them together to make a sandwich.

"I thought they were called nasturtiums," said Piglet timidly, as he went on jumping.

"No," said Pooh. "Not these. These are called mastershalums."

The House at Pooh Corner

Peanut Butter, Bacon, and Honey Sandwiches

For 2 sandwiches: 1 strip crisp bacon, drained
2–3 Tablespoons peanut butter ½ teaspoon honey

Crumble the bacon into the peanut butter and add the honey.
Mix and spread on freshly sliced bread.

Roo was silent for a little while, and then he said, "Shall we eat our sandwiches, Tigger?" And Tigger said, "Yes, where are they?"

The House at Pooh Corner

LUNCHES
AND SUPPERS

"Anyhow," he said, "it is nearly Luncheon Time."

So he went home for it.

Winnie-the-Pooh

Tomato Soup

(*Yield: 4 servings*)

4 cups tomatoes, 2 #1 cans or,
   if fresh, cut in pieces
2 fresh scallions, finely cut,
   stem and bulb
      or
1 small onion, finely diced
¼ teaspoon dried thyme (½
   teaspoon fresh)

½ teaspoon dried basil
   (1 teaspoon fresh)
½ teaspoon parsley, finely
   chopped
½–1 teaspoon salt
⅛ teaspoon pepper
½ cup heavy cream

Simmer the tomatoes, scallions, thyme, basil, parsley, salt and pepper together for ½ hour. Add ½ cup of water or tomato juice (if the fresh tomatoes are not juicy).

Heat but do not boil the cream in a large saucepan.

Strain the tomato soup through a sieve slowly into the cream, stirring all the time.

This is delicious hot or ice cold.

> "It's snowing still," said Eeyore gloomily.
> "So it is."
> "*And* freezing."
> "Is it?"
> "Yes," said Eeyore. "However," he said, brightening up a little, "we haven't had an earthquake lately."
>
> *The House at Pooh Corner*

Pea-Bean Alphabet Soup

(Yield: 10–11 servings, approximately)

3 Tablespoons each of dried beans, such as red, Great Northern, garbanzos, pintos, or black for a total of 15 Tablespoons

5 Tablespoons lentils

4 Tablespoons split peas, green or yellow

2 quarts water

1 beef bone, marrow or shank

1 ham bone with a little ham on it

1 large yellow onion, diced

2 cups canned tomatoes

6 sprigs parsley, chopped fine, leaves and stems

½ cup alphabet noodles

Salt and pepper to taste

Soak the beans and peas in water to cover for 3 hours or longer.

Drain and rinse with fresh water.

Cover with the 2 quarts of water and add the meat bones, onion, tomatoes, and parsley in a Dutch oven or a pot with a tight-fitting lid.

Simmer until the peas disappear and the beans are tender, about 2 hours.

During the last 10 minutes of simmering, add the alphabet noodles.

Put in plenty of P's for Pooh and Piglet and the initials or letters of your own name.

Remove the bones and any meat that has cooked free of them. Dice the meat and add to the soup.

"Do you know what this is?"

"No," said Piglet.

"It's an A."

"Oh," said Piglet.

"Not O, A," said Eeyore severely. "Can't you *hear*, or do you think you have more education than Christopher Robin?"

The House at Pooh Corner

Quick Corn and Shrimp Chowder

(Yield: approximately 4–5 cups)

1 Tablespoon butter or margarine
1 medium onion, diced, to make ⅔ cup
1 cup fresh or bottled clam juice
¼ teaspoon dried thyme
1 17-ounce can cream-style corn
1 boiled potato, diced, about 1 cup

1 cup uncooked, cleaned, fresh or frozen shrimp. (Tuna, cod, halibut or other fish, cooked or fresh, can be used instead of or with shrimp.)
1 cup milk or cream
Salt to taste
Paprika
Finely chopped parsley

Lightly brown the onion in the butter or margarine in a heavy-bottomed pot, 2-quart size or larger.

Add the clam juice, thyme, corn, and diced cooked potato and set over low heat.

Let simmer for 5 minutes.

Add the shrimp, or any other fish, and simmer until the shrimp are pink and tender or the other fish is cooked through.

Add the milk and heat again, this time just to the boil.

Taste to see if the chowder needs salt. Add ¼ teaspoon at a time.

Serve in hot soup bowls. Dust with paprika and decorate with a sprinkle of finely chopped parsley.

Serve with chowder crackers.

"*Could* you ask your friend to do his exercises somewhere else? I shall be having lunch directly, and don't want it bounced on just before I begin. . . ."

The House at Pooh Corner

Hot Potato Salad
with Tuna Fish

(Yield: 4 servings)

3 medium potatoes, unpeeled
¼ cup diced celery
½ cup diced scallions, stem and bulbs, or onion
½ cup diced green pepper
1 Tablespoon butter or margarine with
1 Tablespoon cooking oil
2 Tablespoons cider vinegar

2 Tablespoons salad oil
½ teaspoon lemon juice
2 teaspoons minced parsley
½ teaspoon each of chives and fresh tarragon,
    or
¼ teaspoon dried tarragon
Salt and pepper
1 3½-ounce can tuna, drained and flaked

Wash and boil the potatoes in salted water in a covered pot until tender.

Cool and skin.

In a skillet sauté the celery, scallions or onion, and green

pepper in the butter, or margarine, and cooking oil, until barely soft.

Cut the potatoes, which should measure about 3 cups when thinly sliced, into the top of a double boiler and add the sautéed vegetables.

Mix the vinegar, oil, and lemon juice. Add the parsley, chives, and tarragon. Pour over the potatoes. Stir until thoroughly coated.

Add the tuna and mix thoroughly.

Taste.

Add salt and pepper and either a little more oil, vinegar, or lemon juice to suit your taste. It is impossible to give the exact quantities of salt and pepper, oil, vinegar, and lemon juice as different brands of tuna require different seasonings and have more or less natural oil.

"Rabbit," said Pooh to himself. "I *like* talking to Rabbit. He talks about sensible things. He doesn't use long, difficult words, like Owl. He uses short easy words, like 'What about lunch?' and 'Help yourself, Pooh!' "

The House at Pooh Corner

Haycorn Squash

(*Yield: 2 average servings*)

1 large acorn squash	¼ teaspoon pepper
¼ pound ground beef	1 small tomato, peeled, fresh
2 Tablespoons tomato paste	or canned (optional)
½ teaspoon salt	1 Tablespoon diced green
	pepper

If the squash will not stand, slice a wafer-thin piece off the bottom in one spot.

Cut the top off the squash in a straight cut, even if the top is then lopsided. Scrape out the seeds and keep them.

Mix the ground beef with the other ingredients and fill the squash with it.

Put the squash top back on.

Bake in a 375°F oven until the squash is tender, from 45 minutes to 1¼ hours, depending on the squash.

Squash Seeds: wash and dry the seeds and toast them in the oven while baking the squash. They are done when they are lightly golden. Eat plain or sprinkle with salt.

"I'm planting a haycorn, Pooh, so that it can grow into an oak tree, and have lots of haycorns just out-side the front door instead of having to walk miles and miles, do you see, Pooh?"

The House at Pooh Corner

Lamb Patties with Mint Sauce

2 Tablespoons dried mint
¼ cup cider vinegar
¼ cup water
1 Tablespoon honey

1 lamb patty for each person
Salt and pepper

Put the mint, vinegar, water, and honey in a saucepan and bring it to the boil. Cover and set it on a burner at warm. Do not boil. Let it steep while you cook the patties. Yield: about ½ cup.

Broil, or pan-broil in a skillet without butter or oil, one lamb patty for each person to be served. Sprinkle the top of each patty with salt and a little pepper. When brown on one side, turn, season, and brown on the other.

". . . suppose I get stuck in his front door again, coming out, as I did once when his front door wasn't big enough?"

"Because I *know* I'm not getting fatter, but his front door may be getting thinner."

The House at Pooh Corner

Cottleston Pie

(Preheat oven to 375° F)   *(Yield: 6 servings)*

1 9-inch pie shell baked until firm but not browned
¾ cup bite-size pieces of cooked ham
3 eggs
2 cups whipping cream

¼ teaspoon salt
Grind pepper
Pinch nutmeg
1½ Tablespoons butter cut in tiny dots
½ cup grated cheese (optional)

Bake the pie shell in a preheated oven at 425° F.

To keep the pie shell from sliding down the sides and puffing up at the bottom, prick sides and bottom well with the tines of a fork.

Line the bottom with a double thickness of cheesecloth and cover it with small clean stones, which you have gathered at the beach and washed, or with 1 inch of raw rice. Keep the rice and use it again and again.

Distribute the ham on the bottom of the baked pie shell.

Beat the eggs and cream with the seasonings in a bowl until thoroughly mixed.

Pour on top of the ham.

Scatter the butter dots and cheese, if you use it, on top.

Set on rack in the middle of the oven and bake for 25–30 minutes until Cottleston pie has puffed up and browned.

Serve immediately while piping hot.

Cottleston, Cottleston, Cottleston Pie,
A fly can't bird, but a bird can fly.
Ask me a riddle and I reply:
"Cottleston, Cottleston, Cottleston Pie."
                                    Winnie-the-Pooh

Spinach and Bacon

(Yield: 4 servings)

COLD:

½ pound spinach, washed, drained, and dried
4 strips crisp bacon
1 Tablespoon bacon fat

1 teaspoon salad oil
1 Tablespoon vinegar or lemon juice
Salt to taste

Put the well-dried spinach leaves in a salad bowl.

Toss them with the bacon fat, salad oil, and vinegar or lemon juice.

Crumble the bacon on top. Taste with a little bacon to see if more salt than the bacon gives is necessary.

Add more vinegar or lemon juice to suit your taste.

HOT:

To 1 pound spinach use 2 strips crisp bacon	1 teaspoon or more of lemon juice or cider vinegar Salt to taste

Let the bacon drain and crisp between sheets of paper toweling.

Drain the spinach, which should be cooked quickly in a small amount of water in a heavy-bottomed saucepan, through a colander. Press out all the water and cut it across both ways.

Put the spinach in a serving bowl that has been heated in a warming oven.

Pour the lemon juice or vinegar over it and toss.

Crumble the bacon on top of the spinach.

Served with muffins and butter and honey, fruit, and a glass of milk, this is a fine lunch or supper.

So they went to the Six Pine Trees, and threw fir-cones at each other until they had forgotten what they came for, and they left the basket under the trees and went back to dinner.

The House at Pooh Corner

Creamed Salmon on Crackers

(*Yield: 4 servings*)

1 7-ounce can salmon	2 Tablespoons butter
¼ teaspoon thyme	1½ Tablespoons flour
Salt & pepper	1 cup milk, heated
Paprika	Soda crackers
	Parsley flowerets

Remove the bones and skin from the salmon. Drain and break into pieces in the top of a double boiler. Add the thyme, salt, if the salmon is unsalted, and pepper. Set it in the bottom of the double boiler in hot water. Cover and let it heat.

In a heavy-bottomed saucepan, or a no stick pan, cook the butter and flour together for 2 minutes. Slowly add the heated milk, stirring vigorously all the time. This makes a medium-thick sauce.

Pour it over the salmon in the double boiler.

Heat the soda crackers in the oven. Use 1 large or 2 small for each serving.

Spoon the creamed salmon onto the crackers.

Decorate with paprika and parsley.

. . . Pooh went out to discover the East Pole by himself. Whether he discovered it or not, I forget; but he was so tired when he got home that, in the very middle of his supper, after he had been eating for little more than half-an-hour, he fell fast asleep in his chair, and slept and slept and slept.

Winnie-the-Pooh

Jelly Omelet

2–3 eggs
    Small skillet, 7-inch

1 Tablespoon butter or
   margarine
2 Tablespoons jelly
   Salt and pepper

Break the eggs in a bowl, add a little salt and pepper, and beat with a fork until the yolks and whites are thoroughly mixed.

Heat the skillet with the butter and pour in the beaten eggs.

Keep over low heat. When the bottom of the egg mixture is firm and the top soft but not runny, spoon in the jelly evenly over the back half of the egg surface.

Loosen the egg mixture on the unjellied front half around the edge of the pan. Tip the pan away from you and flip the front half of the egg mixture over the back half.

Let it sit for a minute before serving.

. . . humming to himself in a rather sticky voice, he got up, shook Rabbit lovingly by the paw, and said that he must be going on.

"Must you?" said Rabbit politely.

"Well," said Pooh, "I could stay a little longer if it—if you—" and he tried very hard to look in the direction of the larder.

Winnie-the-Pooh

DESSERT AND
PARTY RECIPES

"Pooh," he said, "Christopher Robin is giving
a party."

"Oh," said Pooh. . . . "Will there be those little
cake things with pink sugar icing?"

Winnie-the-Pooh

Colored Honey

Honey takes coloring even more easily than sugar.

Use vegetable food coloring, the kind you buy to color the icings on cakes and for dying Easter eggs. Food colors come in red, yellow, blue, and green.

Shake or tap the bottle gently so you get one drop at a time. Work up to the color you want.

You can also mix your colors.

You could also color your breakfast honey, one color for each day of the week.

Use small jars with airtight screw tops, so the colored honey can be stored.

. . . his nose told him it was indeed honey, and his tongue came out and began to polish up his mouth, ready for it.

Winnie-the-Pooh

Fruited Honey

Putting whole or sliced fruits "down" in honey can be done ahead of time and they make a delicious dessert.

Use one jar with a tight cover for each kind of fruited honey.

Wash the fruit—whole strawberries, raspberries, blackberries, blueberries, huckleberries; sliced peaches, apricots, cantaloupe, honeydew melon, apples, pears, bananas, grapefruit and orange slices with shredded coconut or a combination of fruit and berries—and fill a clean jar. Pour honey over it to the top of the jar.

Cap it and turn it upside down a few times immediately, and then whenever you think of it during the rest of the day and the next morning.

These will keep for several weeks in the refrigerator.

They can be eaten with a piece of plain cake or a cookie.

So he took his largest pot of honey and escaped with it to a broad branch of his tree, well above the water, and then he climbed down again and escaped with another pot . . . and when the whole Escape was finished, there was Pooh sitting on his branch, dangling his legs, and there, beside him, were ten pots of honey. . . .

Winnie-the-Pooh

Fruit or Berry Whip
After A Happy Afternoon

1 cup heavy cream
1 Tablespoon honey

3 cups mashed fruit or berry pulp: peaches, bananas, nectarines, apricots, strawberries, raspberries, blueberries, huckleberries, or blackberries

Whip the cream until stiff.
Dribble the honey over it.
Fold in the fruit or berry pulp.

Christopher Robin came down from the Forest to the bridge, feeling all sunny and careless, and just as if twice nineteen didn't matter a bit, as it didn't on such a happy afternoon . . .

The House at Pooh Corner

Honey Chocolate Pie

(*Preheat oven to 375° F*)

1 9-inch pie shell, uncooked
4 ounces semisweet chocolate
¼ cup butter (2 ounces)
1 14½-ounce can evaporated milk
½ cup honey

1 cup sugar
3 Tablespoons cornstarch
¼ teaspoon salt
2 large eggs, beaten
½ cup whipping cream

Buy a ready-made pie shell or make your own from any standard recipe or any of the piecrust mixes. Line the piepan with the pastry before starting the honey-chocolate mixture.

Melt the chocolate and butter in the top of a double boiler.

When melted, remove from the heat and blend in the evaporated milk, stirring all the time.

In a mixing bowl blend together the honey, sugar, cornstarch, and salt

Beat in the eggs.

Add this mixture to the chocolate mixture slowly, beating all the time.

Pour this filling into the waiting pie shell.

Bake the pie uncovered for 40 minutes.

Then cover it lightly with aluminum foil and bake it 20 minutes more until the top is puffed. Cracks sometimes show in the center.

Cool for an hour and then refrigerate.

Serve cold with whipped cream piled on it.

Dribble a thin trickle of honey beads over the whipped cream.

This is very rich and sweet, so bake it when you'll be having several friends in for lunch or supper or a dessert party.

When they had all nearly eaten enough, Christopher Robin banged on the table with his spoon, and everybody stopped talking and was very silent, except Roo who was just finishing a loud attack of hiccups and trying to look as if it was one of Rabbit's relations.

Winnie-the-Pooh

Cherry Pie

1 9-inch pie shell
½ cup sugar
3 Tablespoons cornstarch
½ teaspoon salt
Cherry juice from a # 1 can of red tart cherries and water to make 1 cup
Red food coloring
1 3-ounce package cream cheese
1 Tablespoon honey
1 cup whipping cream

This is a 1-crust pie. Prick it well with a fork, sides and bottom, and bake until done according to the directions on the piecrust mix or your recipe. Let it cool while you prepare the filling. It should be cold when you add the filling.

FILLING: Combine and cook together until the mixture boils and thickens over low heat the sugar, cornstarch, salt, and cherry juice.

When the mixture is thick, pour in the cherries.

Add a few drops of red food coloring and stir until it is cherry red all over.

Set this aside off the heat.

Blend together the cream cheese and honey.

Add the cherry mixture to this slowly and beat them together until thoroughly combined.

When the filling is cool, whip ½ cup cream. Fold it into the cherry mixture.

Pour the mixture into the cold baked pie shell, scraping the bowl with a rubber spatula or a spoon.

Chill at least 4–5 hours. This is better if chilled 8 hours.

When ready to serve, whip the remaining ½ cup cream and top the pie with it.

Pooh didn't mind for himself, but when he thought of all the honey the bees wouldn't be making, a cold and misty day always made him feel sorry for them.

The House at Pooh Corner

Blueberry Pie

(*Preheat oven to 450° F*)

Dough for a 2-crust pie
(1 package of ready-mix)
3½ cups fresh blueberries
or
3 15-ounce cans of wild blueberries, well drained

10 white grapes, washed and
seeded
1 Tablespoon flour
3 Tablespoons sugar
Pinch salt

Follow the directions on the ready-mix piecrust. Divide the dough in two balls, one larger than the other.

Roll out the larger ball between sheets of wax paper for a bottom crust and line your 9-inch pie plate.

Roll out the smaller ball of dough and leave it ready for cutting.

Dredge the berries and grapes very lightly in the flour.

Put them in the pie shell and sprinkle with the sugar and salt.

The berries should look as though a light snow had fallen on them.

Cut the waiting dough in Woozle and Wizzle tracks and run them across or over the blueberries.

Or you may cut the remaining dough in strips about ½-inch wide and crisscross them on top of your pie.

Set the pie in a pan with a rim or a skillet to catch the blue-berry juice.

Bake your pie on the middle rack of the hot oven for 40 minutes.

"No," said Pooh, "because it makes different marks. It is either Two Woozles and one, as it might be, Wizzle, or Two, as it might be, Wizzles and one, if so it is, Woozle. Let us continue to follow them."

Winnie-the-Pooh

Hipy Papy Bthuthdth Thuthda
Bthuthdy Cake I

(*Preheat oven to 350° F*)   (*Yield: 16–18 slices*)

1 cup each butter
    and milk
2 cups sugar
	3 cups all-purpose flour,
	    sifted with 3 teaspoons
	    double-acting baking powder
	    and 3 pinches salt (⅛
	    teaspoon)
	4 large eggs

This is also known as a 1, 2, 3, 4 birthday cake. You can see why from the list of ingredients.

Butter and flour a 10-inch tube pan.

Cream the butter and sugar.

Beat in the eggs, one at a time.

Sift the flour with the baking powder and salt and add it alternately with the milk, beginning and ending with the flour to make a cake of fine texture.

Beat for at least 3 minutes or until well blended.

Pour into the buttered and floured tube pan.

Bake for about an hour or until a cake tester or a toothpick, when stuck in the cake an inch from either side, comes out clean.

Let cool about 30 minutes in the pan before turning out on a rack to finish cooling.

This makes a lovely light cake for the youngest and smallest children. It is easy to make. It can be iced or eaten plain or with a sprinkle of powdered sugar or a brush of honey.

If you don't want to ice the cake, it can be made to look very festive with its powdered sugar and with candles, cherries or strawberries, or a few violets, nasturtiums, geranium blossoms, or roses.

Or you can fill the center hole left by the tube with fruit or berry whip, page 81. Be sure the cake has cooled for at least an hour.

So Owl wrote . . . and this is what he wrote:
HIPY PAPY BTHUTHDTH THUTHDA BTHUTHDY

Winnie-the-Pooh

Hipy Papy Bthuthdth Thuthda
Bthuthdy Cake II

(Preheat oven to 375° F)

½ cup butter
½ cup sugar
½ cup honey
2 large eggs, separated
2 cups sifted all-purpose flour
3 teaspoons double-acting
baking powder

¼ teaspoon baking soda
¼ teaspoon salt
½ cup milk
1 teaspoon almond, vanilla, or
lemon extract

Butter and flour two 8-inch cake pans.

Cream the butter with the sugar and honey, adding both gradually until they are absorbed and the mixture is light in texture.

Add the egg yolks one at a time, beating well after each.

Sift the flour with the baking powder, soda, and salt and

add it to the butter-egg yolk mixture alternately with the milk and flavoring, beginning and ending with the flour for a cake of fine texture.

Beat the egg whites until stiff so that they keep their shape and gently fold into the cake batter. Do not beat.

Pour the cake batter into the buttered and floured cake pans, half full.

Put them on the middle shelf of the preheated oven and bake for about 30 minutes or until a cake tester or knife blade stuck into the center of each layer comes out clean.

Let the cakes cool for about 5 minutes. They will pull away from the sides of the pans. Turn them over on a cake rack and tap the bottom of the pans to remove the layers.

Do not fill or frost until they have cooled for at least an hour.

For icings, see the next two pages or use the fruit and berry whip.

"You ought to write *A Happy Birthday* on it."
Winnie-the-Pooh

Pink Honey Buttercream Frosting

2 Tablespoons honey
Red food coloring
1 pound (1 box) confectioners'
sugar, sifted if lumpy

½ cup (¼ pound or 1 stick)
butter or margarine, soft
½ teaspoon salt
2–3 Tablespoons milk

Add a few drops of red food coloring to the honey to make a deep pink.

Cream 1 cup of the confectioners' sugar with the butter.

Add the salt, pink honey, and the rest of the confectioners' sugar alternately with the milk.

Adjust the coloring to get the shade of pink you want by adding more red food coloring.

If the frosting is not of the right spreading consistency, add a little more milk until it is.

This will fill and frost two 9-inch layers adequately; two 8-inch layers generously.

"Look at the birthday cake. Candles and pink sugar."

Winnie-the-Pooh

Honey Chocolate Icing

1 ounce (1 square)   2 Tablespoons honey
  semisweet chocolate   3 Tablespoons butter

This is enough to ice two or three cupcakes. To do a 2-layer cake multiply the ingredients by 5, or by 4 for Bthuthdy Cake I.

Melt and stir the chocolate, honey, and butter over hot water in the top of a double boiler.

Let it cool enough to spread on your cake. If you are in a hurry, set it in a bowl of ice cubes and cold water and stir until cool.

If it stiffens, heat it up again over hot water.

After icing, refrigerate cake until about 20 minutes before serving.

"A lick of honey," murmured Bear to himself, "or —or not, as the case may be."

Winnie-the-Pooh

Honey Custard

2 egg yolks	2 egg whites
1 Tablespoon honey	Pinch salt
Grated rind of ½ lemon	2–3 drops vanilla, almond, or mint extract

Beat the egg yolks with the honey.

Add the grated lemon rind.

Beat the egg whites until stiff. Add a pinch of salt.

Fold the stiffly beaten egg whites into the honey-custard mixture.

Add the flavoring.

Spoon into 4 small custard cups and serve.

"What do you like doing best in the world, Pooh?"

"Well," said Pooh, "what I like best——" and then he had to stop and think. Because although Eating Honey *was* a very good thing to do, there was a moment just before you began to eat it which was better than when you were, but he didn't know what it was called.

The House at Pooh Corner

CHRISTMAS
SPECIALTIES

On Tuesday, when it hails and snows,
The feeling on me grows and grows. . .
Winnie-the-Pooh

Christmas Honey Wafers

(Preheat oven to 300°F)   *(Yield: about 2½ dozen)*

1 cup chopped nutmeats
½ cup honey
⅓ cup molasses
½ cup butter or margarine

1 scant cup all-purpose flour
½ cup sugar
1 Tablespoon cinnamon or
   ginger

Butter cookie sheets well.

Break or chop the nutmeats into medium-size pieces.

Heat the honey and molasses to the boiling point but do not boil.

Add the butter, melt and remove from heat.

In a mixing bowl measure out and sift the flour with the sugar and cinnamon or ginger. Add the nutmeats.

Stirring constantly, add the spiced flour mixture and the nutmeats to the sweetened butter.

Drop the cookies from a teaspoon 3 inches apart and bake them for 15 minutes.

Remove from oven and let sit for a minute before removing with a broad spatula.

To make wafer sticks or ice cream cones, wrap them while still warm around the handle of a wooden spoon. For full directions, see Christmas Nut Cookies, page 98.

> "Well," said Eeyore that afternoon, when he saw them all walking up to his house, "this *is* a surprise. Am *I* asked too?"
>
> *The House at Pooh Corner*

Christmas Nut Cookies

(*Preheat oven to 300° F*) (*Yield: about 4 dozen*)

1 cup nuts, broken into large pieces
3 Tablespoons butter or margarine, at room temperature
1 scant cup dark brown sugar
2 Tablespoons honey
1 egg
2 Tablespoons flour
¼ teaspoon salt, if nuts are unsalted

Pecans, filberts, walnuts, or mixed nuts without peanuts, coarsely chopped, are good for these cookies. If salted nuts are used, dust off as much salt as possible with a paper towel.

Heavily grease the cookie sheets.

By hand or electric mixer:

Cream the soft butter, brown sugar, and honey together.

Add the egg and flour.

Beat until thoroughly blended.

Add the nuts and beat again.

In a blender: Put all ingredients except the nuts in the blender at once and beat on "Blend" or high. Add the nuts and continue blending only until nuts are coarsely chopped.

Beat the batter before each batch of cookies is to be made to distribute the nuts evenly.

The batter should drop easily from a teaspoon. Thin it with a little water if it is too thick. You will get a chewy cookie adding no water and crisper and lacier ones if you use 1–2 teaspoons of water.

Drop by the ½ teaspoon onto the heavily greased cookie sheet, 5 inches apart.

Bake for 10–12 minutes. Let cool a minute or two.

Remove from the cookie sheets with the back of the spatula, and let them cool, unstacked and not touching at their edges, on wire racks.

Cornucopias: Bake the cookies for 4–5 minutes at 350°F and let them cool for only a second before removing them with a spatula. Have a wooden spoon handy and curl the cookies around the handle while they are still warm. The cornucopias may be filled with whipped cream sweetened with a dribble of honey. The honey may be colored red and green, see Colored Honey, page 79.

Ice Cream Cones: Make these exactly as you do the cornucopias but drop the cookie batter from a tablespoon and wrap them a little more loosely than you do the cornucopias. Pinch the bottoms together to make them drip-proof.

Hardening: If the cookies harden while you're making the cornucopias or ice cream cones, return them to the oven for a minute or two. Unless they are warm, they become too brittle to curl around the wooden handle.

I
And all your friends
Sends—
(*Very awkward this, it keeps
   going wrong*)
Well, anyhow, we send
   Our love
END.
The House at Pooh Corner

Honey Gingerbread Cookies

(*Preheat oven to 350° F*)

(*Yield: about 2½ dozen 3-inch round cookies*)

½ cup sugar
3 cups sifted all-purpose flour
2 teaspoons baking soda
1 teaspoon salt
2 teaspoons powdered ginger

2 teaspoons cinnamon
½ teaspoon each powdered cloves and nutmeg
½ pound butter or margarine cut into dots
½ cup honey

Sift the sugar, flour, baking soda, salt, ginger, cinnamon, cloves, and nutmeg together into a mixing bowl.

Work the dots of butter into the dry ingredients with your fingertips.

When thoroughly worked in, add the honey and stir until blended.

Refrigerate for an hour, or longer if possible.

Roll the dough out about ⅛-inch thick on a floured board or between sheets of waxed paper.

Cut it into the shapes of Gingerbread Men or Houses or Pooh shapes made from tracings of the Pooh drawings.

Bake for 12 to 15 minutes on a cookie sheet in the preheated oven.

Remove from oven and, after a minute, from cookie sheet with a spatula to cool on cake racks.

He made up a little hum that very morning as he was doing his Stoutness Exercises in front of the glass:
Tra-la-la, tra-la-la,
Tra-la-la, tra-la-la,
Rum-tum-tiddle-um-tum

Winnie-the-Pooh

Honey Oatmeal Cookies

(Preheat oven to 350° F)   *(Yield: 2½-3 dozen, depending on amount of fruits, nuts, or chocolate added)*

2 Tablespoons butter or margarine
1 Tablespoon liquid shortening
½ cup brown sugar
¼ cup honey
1 egg
1 Tablespoon water

½ cup all-purpose flour, sifted
½ teaspoon salt
¼ teaspoon baking soda
1½ cups rolled oats
Any amount you choose of the following: chopped dates, figs, apples, raisins, currants, chocolate chips, chopped nuts, or a mixture of these

Butter cookie sheets.

The butter or margarine should be at room temperature.

Blend the butter, liquid shortening, brown sugar, honey, egg, and water thoroughly.

Sift together the sifted flour, salt, and baking soda.

Add the rolled oats.

Stir and blend the oats mixture with the liquid mixture.

Divide the cookie mixture into as many bowls as you need for the fruits, nuts, etc.

Add the fruits or nuts or chocolate or your own combination of these to each bowl and mix into batter.

Drop by the heaping teaspoon onto the greased cookie sheets. Bake for 12–15 minutes.

Remove with a spatula to cool, not touching, on a wire rack or foil.

"Nobody knows anything about this," he went on. "This is a Surprise."

The House at Pooh Corner

Coconut Honey Cookies

(*Preheat oven to 350° F*)   (*Yield: about 2 dozen*)

2 Tablespoons honey
¼ cup peanut butter
¼ teaspoon salt

3 squares (3 ounces) semisweet chocolate
1 cup condensed milk
1½ cups shredded coconut (4-
ounce can)

Butter cookie sheets.

Mix the honey with the peanut butter and salt and let them sit in the bowl.

Melt the chocolate in the top of a double boiler with the condensed milk.

Pour the milk chocolate into the honey peanut butter.

Add the shredded coconut.

Drop by the heaping teaspoonful about an inch apart onto the cookie sheets.

Bake for 10–12 minutes.

Remove from the cookie sheet with a spatula while the cookies are still warm.

Cool on a wire rack.

" . . . just a mouthful of condensed milk or whatnot, with perhaps a lick of honey——"

Winnie-the-Pooh

104

Honey Milk Chocolate Fudge

(Yield: a little over 2 pounds)

18 ounces semisweet chocolate
¼ teaspoon salt
1½ teaspoons honey

1⅓ cups condensed milk (15-ounce can)
½ cup coarsely chopped nut-meats

Butter or line an 8-inch square pan or the equivalent, with wax paper or foil.

Melt the chocolate in the top of a double boiler over hot water.

Stir and remove from the heat when melted.

Add the salt, honey, and condensed milk.

Stir to make a smooth mixture.

If you like, add the nutmeats.

Pour the fudge into the prepared pan.

Spread it evenly in the pan and smoothe the top.

If you'd like, decorate it with nutmeats an inch apart.

Refrigerate for at least 2 hours.

Cut into squares.

Keep refrigerated but remove from refrigeration about 20 minutes before serving.

> On Thursday when it starts to freeze
> And hoar-frost twinkles on the trees
> How very readily one sees
> That these are whose—but whose are these?
> *Winnie-the-Pooh*

Honey Eggnog

(*Yield: 1 serving*)

1 egg, white and yolk separated   ⅔ cup milk
   Pinch salt   Food coloring or fruit syrup
2 Tablespoons honey

Beat the egg white and add the salt as the white begins to froth. Beat until stiff. Set aside.

Beat the honey and the yolk of the egg together until blended. Heat ⅔ cup milk until very hot but not boiling.

Add a little of the hot milk to the honey-egg yolk mixture and beat.

Add the rest of the hot milk gradually, beating all the time. Fold in the egg white.

You may add some food coloring to the honey or some fruit syrup, raspberry, strawberry, or other flavors.

"It's a comforting sort of thing to have,"
said Christopher Robin . . .

The House at Pooh Corner

Easy Christmas Candy

(*Preheat oven to 300° F*)   (*Yield: 15–18 pieces*)

¼ cup honey
    Food coloring, red and green
¼ cup (½ stick 2 ounces)
    butter or margarine

1 cup filberts or other nuts,
    finely ground
½ teaspoon vanilla extract

If you like, you may color the honey, half red and half of it green, or use it plain. Color and set aside.

Heat a 1-quart casserole until very hot. Be sure to use heavy potholders or asbestos mitts.

Melt the butter in it.

Add the ground nuts and vanilla flavoring.

Stir together until the nuts are well coated with the butter.

Add the honey and beat again until thoroughly mixed.

Refrigerate.

When the mixture is cool enough to handle, shape it into balls or sticks, a Tablespoon at a time. Store the candies on a tray, not touching, and tightly covered over with plastic wrap in the refrigerator, or wrap each candy separately.

This is delicious candy that also makes a lovely stuffing for pitted dates.

Variation: instead of butter or margarine, melt ¼ cup of peanut butter in your casserole and add 1 cup of ground peanuts and ¼ cup of plain honey. Proceed as above.

> "And I know it *seems* easy," said Piglet to himself, "but it isn't *everyone* who could do it."
>
> *The House at Pooh Corner*

HONEY
SAUCES

Isn't it funny
How a bear likes honey?
Buzz! Buzz! Buzz!
I wonder why he does?

Winnie-the-Pooh

Honey Chocolate Sauce

(*Yield: ¾ cup*)

4 squares (4 ounces) semisweet
chocolate
4 Tablespoons water

¼ cup honey
2 Tablespoons butter
1 screw-top jar

Melt the chocolate in the water over low heat in a heavy-bottomed saucepan.

Simmer it for 3 minutes.

Remove from the heat and stir in the honey and the butter.

Beat it hard. Then:

1. Pour it over ice cream, cake, cream cakes, plain rice pudding.

2. Add 2 Tablespoons of the sauce to a glass of warm milk and stir.

3. Put sauce in an airtight jar. It will keep in the refrigerator or in a cool place for a week or more. Reheat but do not boil if you want the sauce warm again.

"It's like this," he said. "When you go after honey with a balloon, the great thing is not to let the bees know you're coming."

Winnie-the-Pooh

Honey Nut Butter

1 cup fresh or salted nutmeats
1 Tablespoon soft butter
1 Tablespoon honey

1 Tablespoon dextrose
or 1 Tablespoon peanut oil
¼ teaspoon salt if fresh
nutmeats are used
1 screw-top jar

Buy the dextrose at your drugstore.

Make this with almonds, filberts, cashews, pecans, walnuts, or mixed nuts, fresh or salted. Brush off what salt you can if the nutmeats are heavily salted. Add a little salt to the fresh.

Blanch and squeeze off the skins of almonds.

Chop the nutmeats, coarse or fine, in a blender or by hand. Do a few at a time.

Add the other ingredients together and beat until thoroughly blended.

Store in a tightly capped jar and refrigerate. We have never been able to find out how long this will keep because it is always eaten up within a day or two. Of course you can make two, three, or four times as much as this recipe if you want to.

Very good in sandwiches, on crackers (triple layers are good), for picnics, Expotitions, smackerels, teas, lunches, and suppers.

"That's right," said Eeyore. "Sing. Umty-tiddly, umty-too. Here we go gathering Nuts and May. Enjoy yourself!"

Winnie-the-Pooh

Honey Sauce I

1 cup honey ½ cup cream

Heat but do not boil the honey in a double boiler or heavy-bottomed saucepan.

Remove from the heat and slowly stir in the cream.

Blend thoroughly.

Use on cereals, pancakes, waffles, French toast, ice cream, cake, apple pie, tarts, or other desserts.

Store in a screw-top jar and refrigerate, if any is left over.

Winnie-the-Pooh woke up suddenly in the middle of the night and listened. Then he got out of bed, and lit his candle, and stumped across the room to see if anybody was trying to get into his honey-cupboard, and they weren't, so he stumped back again, blew out his candle, and got into bed.

The House at Pooh Corner

Honey Sauce II

1 Tablespoon unsweetened   ⅓ cup honey
    fruit or berry juice   ¼ cup condensed milk

Combine the ingredients and whip until blended.
Delicious as a dessert or as a topping on a dessert.
Store in a screw-top jar in the refrigerator.

"That's funny," he thought. "I know I had a jar
of honey there. A full jar, full of honey right up to the
top, and it had HUNNY written on it, so that I
should know it was honey. That's very funny."

Winnie-the-Pooh

A Recipe for Getting Thin

"How long does getting thin take?"
asked Pooh anxiously.

Winnie-the-Pooh

Index

A. A. MILNE was born in England in 1882, studied at Westminster School and Cambridge University, and for several years was an editor of *Punch*. In 1924 he wrote *When We Were Very Young*, a book of verse dedicated to his only son, Christopher Robin Milne. In 1926 *Winnie-the-Pooh*, which contains the first ten Pooh stories, was published, followed in 1927 by another book of verse, *Now We Are Six*. In 1928 more Pooh stories appeared in *The House at Pooh Corner*. Milne died in 1956.

VIRGINIA H. ELLISON grew up near Poughkeepsie, New York, and was graduated from Vassar College. She lives in Stamford, Connecticut, and has two grown sons. Mrs. Ellison has been an editor and writer for a number of years. Her first Pooh-inspired book, *The Pooh Cook Book*, a collection of original recipes for all occasions, was published in 1969.

ERNEST H. SHEPARD was born in 1879 and lives in Sussex, England. He illustrated all four of the Pooh books, and it is difficult to think of Pooh and his friends apart from Shepard's marvelous drawings. He also illustrated another children's classic, *The Wind in the Willows*, by Kenneth Grahame, as well as several stories of his own.

GRAMBS MILLER, who was born in Peking, China, of American parents, did the charming pen-and-ink explanatory drawings. She came to the United States to study art when she was seventeen, and now illustrates books for both adults and children. Miss Miller and her writer-husband live in New York City.